Travels of Marco

Also by Mark Levine

Debt
Enola Gay
The Wilds

Travels of Marco

Mark Levine

Four Way Books
Tribeca

Please direct all inquiries to:
Editorial Office
Four Way Books
POB 535, Village Station
New York, NY 10014
www.fourwaybooks.com

Library of Congress Cataloging-in-Publication Data

Levine, Mark, 1965-
[Poems. Selections]
Travels of Marco / by Mark Levine.
pages cm
ISBN 978-1-935536-70-3 (pbk. : alk. paper)
I. Title.
PS3562.E8978A6 2016082
811'.54--dc23

2015028574

This book is manufactured in the United States of America and printed on acid-free paper.

Four Way Books is a not-for-profit literary press. We are grateful for the assistance
we receive from individual donors, public arts agencies, and private foundations.

This publication is made possible with public funds from the National Endowment for the Arts

and from the New York State Council on the Arts, a state agency.

[clmp]

We are a proud member of the Community of Literary Magazines and Presses.

Distributed by University Press of New England
One Court Street, Lebanon, NH 03766

For Everett and Gideon

Contents

The man is gone

—George Herbert

1

Cave

I took my boy to hear an echo.
He wanted to hear one. I wanted him to.

We wended through a half-formed unintelligible
brushy wood to a place I knew called "cave."

It had openings at both ends
and could be seen through, not into.

Nor was it a tunnel, strictly, though it passed
through the ground, though it went somewhere.

It was like stepping into a telescope
unseen, into the dark distorted center.

The walls were arched and laid with glazed tiles,
orange, aqua, muddy green and so

streaked with nervous lines where water had run down,
where water must have trellised down still.

It was not clean. It smelled of piss.
Chicken bones, empties, old rubbers, mold.

Echo, I called. So did my boy.
But his voice was small—birdscratch—it

got all lost inside the echo my voice made;
pale echo, barely one.

That was when I had a boy.
I'm quite sure I did.
I wanted one, back then, when I had something to offer,
when I wasn't in this place, where light passes through me,
when I wasn't like this,
which is what,
when I wanted one,
as he, poor boy, wanted me.

Employment

I had a calling.
I took the call.
It was all I could do to follow the voice streaming into me
Like traffic on the runway where I lay
Down to gather.
I had a calling. I heard the geese bleat
In the firmament as they migrated
Into the jet's jets. ✓
And could I have foreseen that falling
I could have fallen too
Rather than being sutured to the bottomless
Freeze-out lake.
For it is fine to lie within one's borrowed blankets ← like being under water
Looking up at the
Dropped ceiling coming down.
For at the moment I am counting holes
In the sound-absorbing tiles
Keeping a running record of the interlocutor's
Chides.
I feel at one with extinction
By my own hand
(Inner hand)
Though once there were many of my kind
Flocking inland, or perhaps
It felt that way.

Rue

I was a traveler in my day
a business traveler, territorial
in the grassy gaps.
I sold bonds
to clients hungry for bonds
in the boundless sales call
door to door among
"folks."
It was a job
I was born with.
I had a heavy sample bag, rubber-
banded stack of calling cards
and leather binder
(embossed)
opening upon a vista of
lamination, obligation
rumination.

I furnished
a nation to the chemical engineers and wives
of Schenectady, New York
over coffee, over roast beef
and piano, a kingdom, a nation, a
principality, landlocked state, aspirational acreage
spiritual fallout hideout.
I showed a picture of my boy
cross-legged in front of a backdrop
of a glaciated hanging valley
deep in the transaction

among handshakes and signatures
if it came to it
This is my boy, I said
Come to me.

I was a traveler.
Later I inspected
the nickel mines near Sudbury
telling my boy about the endless
sheer black subterranean drop
in the cage.
I was telling the truth
when I knew how to, as I had to
as sales required, as stewardship permitted, long before
disembodiment.
I kept a picture of my boy
in front of a cardboard tree and treehouse platform
tacked to the upholstered
partition above my desk.
Once I brought him to the office.
He stared at himself.
"I had a treehouse then," he said.

Mutter

There is a brand of play called muteness
Beneath the play yard's interlacing branches.

It appeals to children born
Entre deux guerres, whose specialty it is.

It is mutiny; that is, a tongue
Of foreign origin ending in grunts.

One such child uses his tongue
On a frozen fence for the embrace of it

For the mutating appendage makes of speech
A combat; an internment.

There is a brand of child assisted to the play yard
By his keeper fussing with his zipper.

Yes, it is cold in the high hemisphere
And nothing will be the death of him

As he sets hard sweets on his tongue
He neither chews nor swallows.

Such children can never swing too freely
From the elm's loping barkless arm.

It is mutual. There is smoke on the air, tarry,
Commuting the industry on high

As the children simmer within
Their word-cloud.

And someone or something is calling them home
A familiar voice, if they have one.

Bicycle

When I see a man moving
on a bicycle, I wish to
be on a bicycle, myself.
But my machine, simplicity
itself, is ailing and cannot be
flagged down.

 Bi-directional, you see, it
turns on one axis while entering
in the same turn a steep
reversing beyond.

Or strafing sideways, it catches
its rib in a furrow, bucking twice
then discharging its
man.

When I see a man seated in correct
formation on an uninviting wedge
atop an irregular triangle
of coarsely sutured steel tube,
my sight moves with him
towards the dusky pollen-choked periphery
while my body, rider, stays put.

I do not stray from my stall, nor may I rest
among the bent and ill-shaped
brackets, riddles of transmission,
tapering time-worn steering apparatus.

For despite my efforts to constrain
the front-facing wheel's vaguely
warped forward rotation
(more out of true than not)
my bicycle is removing
its man from sight.

I would have thought I would have been
a bicyclist among men,
climbing on in a leaping start
and heaving along sodden banks
into the shallow swift-flowing stream,
nearly perfectly weightless, fully
at liberty to get on with my
hesitating ride, even
in the long years I had no bicycle,
even when my legs were most curbed.

And as I rode,
stupid infant pleasure returned me
to my body's bicycle;
and I rode until pain made
my bicycle invisible.

Logger

What do you say, new you?
I say I am at a remove.
The boys came yesterday to take my chair.
They succeeded, technically (storm troopers);
yet the soul stayed on, in its own soil.
If I could envision, I would follow
the old logger dragging his felled
tree through winter woods by its chain
until he reaches a river, yellow banks heaped
with logs waiting to spill downstream
among drifts of chewed ice.
Day done.
Then, then it's a long way back to camp
not much sky left in the gaps
where trees once were.
And this path just one among others crossing
halting and going on
illegible and new snow
sweeping over the slash.
Yet he can't not find his way
not make it back.
Wherever he settles
beneath an old lean-to
wherever he sleeps he
wakes with me.

Smith

As I was saying
My belt was in need of repair
At the clasp, thereabouts, useless weapon
I was saying.

For it stood in the rain
Garnering grit in one hand, pants
In the other, clenched, cursing, defenseless mouth
Filling with rain.

For its teeth were in need of repair
Having stamped rivets
In a stiff sash, conjuring
Water to its root system.

And when it grew lost it trod the long gangway's
Sopping boards, pants at heels, speaking
These words to itself
As a gun does.

I had a trade, said my man, honing tools
On the old rack, said my man
Filing sorts, scouring forms
Having a use. Regard:

Tip passes through buckle and retracts.
Pin enters punch hole.
Tip reverses self once more.
Through the loop. Tighter. Again. Once more.

Market

Money changed hands. It's how we came to be
Came to be planted here in the mortar
In the miniature cash forest
Aster greenwood ficus hemlock
Taproot stipe calyx anther in the
Mortal hereafter
Hearing hands making money change.

Speak up. I can't hear you.
There's something wrong with your voice.
You're speaking too fast. Slow up.
Speak into the currency.
It wants to bone you. It wants to receive
Your warmth in its coffers.
Listen up. I've a fee to see to
A toll-man a drawbridge. Open up.
Close up. You have a cross bite
In your crown, palate-ax.
Bite down. Bite my ball
Bearing interest.

I'm a businessman. I own a plant.
I bid for it, bought it, soiled it, drowned it
Tilled it, scolded it, heaved into it, stole from it
Wept unto it
A token in its behalf, suffered a stem

To rise in it
To market, to market
In my dirty jumpsuit
Worthlessness.

Took

It took a truck
to put him back
among the fixtures
and floral tinctures
of his nook
(wormhole).
It took a train
stoking round
the settling pond
to get him word
of the regard
the idle moon
held him in
coming clean
as a clay pipe.
That was his rope.

      That was his rape.
      He grappled his man
      from heel to hind
      the way a pencil
      steered its lead
      up a lordly sycamore.
      His other vehicle
      (two-ton tricycle)
      bore his load
      to the underpass

while an avalanche
took him below
into wetter
tiers.

No making it better.
He lost his next
best boot, implausible
eyelets and nodes.
His fretless junk
(dolphin, lute)
took to the tides
in the fusty hold
of a tanker, supertanker
echo-monger.
It was late as late.
A wagon prowled
at large in the marl
angry for its mule.

All the while
I watched him turning
through my opening
(manhole)
distant, wavering.
He was the third
person of my speech

pathology ward
to elope
hand on gyroscope
on his lonely vigil.
Sundown, countdown.
Away he drove.
He took the wheel
like a vapor trail.
He was the ugly
man in my depot.

Metaphysical

On a lighter note, I've gotten lighter.
I swell with air, then discharge and contract.
The discharge can be wiped or left just so
In the gallery whose task is to preserve
(Reserve, reverse, revert);
The conjugal gallery.
On a lighter note, I lost a finger, most of one.
That was long enough ago. I saved the ring.
And hung it round my throat, to think on Her
Who ventured hence and left me lighter, so.
—And lighter, still, for the sheer thought
Of the added ounces of Her embalmed soul
Has fled me down the dirty well.
I see myself swimming, for survival's sake.
I see the fogged waters filling my eyes.
Yet I look on, though I am prone to panic
In the deeps, for I cannot swim,
Not one fucking stroke; yet I cannot drown,
My emptiness will not
Provide it.

Dance

Old man is done. Here I am dancing
  Dancing in my own step, as others skirt by
Wheel by, are jerked by
    By their loose lashes
Here I am ringed round
  Primate
    Solo dancer
  Stalking a window like a reasoning housefly
In a hexagonal mirror
  An ambulette. I do not dance
    As I danced in prior light
Under a name (Aron)
  A pair of mynahs vying for my
    Flame on each shoulder
White wolf, wonder-working rod
  Cloud spiller
That dance is but done, lord.

  Young man is done. It was not me, was never
    Astride Niagara Falls (Canada)
  In a fiery spume of my own singeing
  Making words, when I had some
When my dance was
    Romancing me
Upon the blunt windshield
    For all to weep.
It may be I've bent to sacrifice
  A step or two lately
As I am empty as a flue

As my adhesive strip
Has left me palely tottering
No hoist to crank forth
No partner boosting old boy's jizz, no
Heedful vengeful god within.

Nails

When I was living here
I had a pair of scissors
Children's scissors, blunt ones,
Only the tips of my thumb
And forefinger fit
While the blades, pivoting,
Slipped together and parted.
They cut a sun from the sky,
And another sun,
And a looming leafless tree
Leaned in the opening
A plane steered through
In a hush, gliding, but
Agitated, clipping a wing.

When I was here, living,
I carried a square of soft
Cloth in my shirt pocket
Among pencils and stained
Business cards.
The cloth was blue lines
And white boxes, like
Worn graph paper, and
Sometimes I jotted a number
On it, or an unusual name
To look up on my return.
When I spilled, I wiped with it.

My eye was watery then.
I had an injured finger then
Bound in the cloth.

When I sold nails
For a living, small one,
I could be found here
On a stool, by the counter,
When I was in work boots
With my customer, in overalls,
With safety glasses, beneath a window,
Near the noise of gas trucks
Idling, keeping the store.
The planks were spreading,
The inventory growing and
Receding, like a nail in the elbow
Of a knotted tree,
In its shade in its porous skin.

The inventory was a living
Thing, slatted fruit crates
On the far wall packed with
Carpet tacks, gutter spikes, brads,
Screw shanks, ring shanks,
Bulletheads, lost-heads, stigs,
When I was living near
The old crusher,

When I was a living
Historical being,
In a storehouse near the lakeshore,
When I slept in a bunk,
Sometimes the bottom
Or above, when
I was a repository,
When I sold nails.

2

Travels of Marco

I was in Asia Minor
in pursuit of distant honor
in a suit of finest armor
in a forest of pine or
planks. I was not lost. Regina
(my sextant) stared into the refiner's
flare as evening grew maligner.

    I was in Kazakhstan
    collecting rarest poppies. My capstan
    gave out. I could no more withstand
    the tides than fall to the rattan
    mat like Tristan
    sailing emptily to his mutant
    island.

        I was in greater Ghana
        harvesting marijuana
        with soul-strafing Tatiana,
        the local swan—a
        mortal one, a
        prize among the fauna.
        (There should have been a lawn a-

            gainst her.) You see, I was in Corinth
            fabricating synth-
            etic absinthe.
            I was adamant. The
            trophy I chased for the ninth

night of days was Cynth
-ia, succumbing at the plinth.

Then to Argentina
I set forth with Ekaterina
a diminishing ballerina.
She pled for fina-
steride, having seen a
parrot turn bright green u-
pon my mythic ocarina.

I was in Tel Aviv.
Viv-
ian (my pigeon) and I were feve
-rish from bouts of griev-
ous liv-
er malaise. We must have been naive
-r than a hibernal beave

-r, for soon I was in Canada
as ever. Had no plan; not a
home to hide in, nothing human. Ada
(vulgar bird) went wan, bade a
screeching goodnight to her one God, a
soapstone strap-on. Alone, I ran a do-
zen tests: None truer, none sadder.

Bird

That day I was reliving
The elements with my fellow residents
Of the aged tenement
On Rue Clémond, somewhat submerged
In cement, still setting.
It was the former neighborhood
Forevermore.
Reliving was the living thing
Stirring a wheel or two on the ward
Where words once were:
Such was daily tenancy
Annually for a decade.
But don't you worry, mockingbird,
Soon I will have slept.

And such was truancy
For it was true the shadows had grown longer
Without my showing up in the keeper's ledger.
And I had rather had
(I told my hind)
My punishment, weathered board
Across my barrenness,
Than not. "No one has died of it yet"
Though one (Miss Chaffinch)
Died trying.
And it was furthermore once said
I could fill a pair of pants

On my own, both openings,
Without devices.
—But now, winged breed,
I need a change,
Sitting in my stuff
In a drying breeze.

Sirrah, that day I was relieving
Myself of elemental wardrobe,
Blouses, sensible shoes, horsehair underthings,
Zippers, trusses, hat bands,
Tourniquets.
I'd no idea I had held on so long
Until he (Mr. Bohbot) pulled me from
The pyre, girl that I loved. Only
Instinct lives on like a
Sad tree.

It's not that I am not content
With this hostel or trench
With its grassy amenities
Though the eminent local fireflies
Flocking in my garments
Taste like incendiary jelly
(Dew).
And you and I are but
A single hyperkinetic heartbeat

Lighting a jar
Until the muscle gives out.
But do not
Tremble, firebird;
We were only passing through.

Untitled (Mel)

1.

Coming by chance
Upon a mate from those days called Mel
I called him by name at the mall's crossroads
Where two rivers heavy with tailings met
For he was drowning in his chair
A pair of dirty white socks
And private openings open to the air's
Melody.
—"Mel," wrote the skywriter, tarring the moon,
"Maestro of melancholy, manufacturer
Of Finer Ladies Raincoats."

2.

Coming by chance
Upon a mate on the glassy shoals
Of the mall's expanse, Mel tapped
His voice box with reflexive
Volts, finding friction
And spraying bits of sound
Auk Auk,
Behind the old saw mill.
He was its sawyer and he was its mule.
Un-calm man,
Rising from his chair and going hard down
Splashless, by the well's wall.

3.

And I foresaw it all, coming upon my chancy mate
En route to a formidable dappled
Melanoma,
Not a cloud in the mall.
I foreswore the custodian slumping on his shine.
I, four, saw pale Mélisande take a dip
In the fathomless while a mélange
Of EMTs ascended from Sears
With a man-sized board and assorted
Fasteners.

4.

Mel, I called, internally, calling him
By his acronym
For he was scaling the mid-passage
At speed.
He turned his head for once.
For once we studied each other across the valley like
Two birds in a burning tree
All wrapped in leaves.
I never was a good bird since my
Corona was clipped.

Fraction

That wasn't the half of it.
  The third man sat for a quarter hour
  Downing a fifth of Bacardi
   In a shower of ice
   Before emerging from a noodle bar
  At Sixth and Bleecker
   (For it could not be any)
 En route to Film Forum
For a private showing
 Of *The Seventh Seal* and I
  Am distant kin to Burt Bacharach
   Eighth of nine siblings
  Or the second of two depending
  On one's genealogical screws
  Regardless am the only
 Eye still blinking after a proper
Nazi trampling. I'll not see twenty-twenty;
Not twenty-ten; have scrubbed my cataracts
 In a dizzy ravine
 In my forty-sixth summer
 Of premature evacuation, having misplaced my walker
   In an essence of soda water
   And earth to make a bed
   For jackpot winners. But I was about to say
  When Chance came and cut me down with his Wehrmacht
That I was present on the assembly floor
And accountable for the little industrial
Severance of a couple digits
  Leaving me ninety-nine and forty-four hundredths

Clean.
　　I'll never again wish myself back to that state
Sponsored shower as long as I.
　The sixteenth squadron spared my hide
　Emptying its gunwales in me for thirty seconds
　　As I stood frozen on the ladder's twenty-seventh rung and
I like to think some boy's been swinging there
　On the forty-ninth parallel called Heaven
　In the northerly taiga where the shales
　Are asleep in a pharmacological hush
　And when my sinuses clear
What am I.

Bear

We have a problem, bear.
Bear with us, will you,
Won't you, while we scratch our sign
In the declining pine barrens,
Grinding our incisors on late-blooming bear grass
(Orbs).
We chomped an apple at break of day
In the dream we had of sustenance
In the long unbroken sleep
Of brain activity.
It was a pear-shaped apple,
Bodiless, stricken with daylight,
As we drowsed, fifty milligrams
Of slumber upon us,
Upon the word for us (aberrant),
In our hairy suit.
And everywhere the field in which we dug
Was fertile with forage,
Spiky primitive shells, and clusters of mashed fruits,
And the picked-over spires of nearly colorless flowers,
Ocher, dun, giving off
Heavy fermenting bronchial sugars,
As a cloud grew empty over us,
As a process was slowing down in us.

For we were
Fattening into obscurity, bear,
With our one ripening thought
Of you (for what you're worth,

On your rare visits to the surface)
Secreted in our glands.

And we were
Bounding, as in youth, across a muddy inlet
In a disassembling seasonal
Light without pigment
With our lexicon of six or fewer signs;
A place of beginnings.
Hungry, pacing, fidgeting,
Except when we were eating, when
We had no appetite
For this feed, who would eat this,
What would you call this.

For as Carmelita (our keeper) has pointed out,
We may no longer occupy our robes,
For our girth is real, though misunderstood,
Though our legs are like old bamboo.
And we stand five-foot-ten, fully extended,
Which means you must have grown in your absence from us
To loom above us so,
Visitor.
Please do not leave us yet,
We worry you will neglect
(As in all things)
To bury us on waking.

Serpent

I was pent up.
I lived in a penthouse—a rental—
 Bent to its bays with sediment,
  Newsprint, lint, effluents, sentiment.
Fruit flies swarmed the box.
 A history of meat repeated itself
In a radio's cadence in the flowing
Freestanding Oriental tub
I got a good scrubbing in.
Then came an agent, sent
Up by the super to serve
Landlordly papers in a language I glanced
At but no more gathered
 Than a tree gathered
  Its debarking.
I was the elder pentathlete
 Of the premises,
  Spent
 Occupant of a pair of parking slots
  For a trio of unrepentant engines,
  Wondering where my long welcome went.
My man has snapped utilities off
 For punishment overdue,
 For guilty I am
 Of radiant sentience,
Having lived by the people I was born by
Taken from and lived without
 A demi-century and meant it.
 A trove of transient fact

38

Will thaw with me
Lamentably in spring
Coming.
I am losing my hold, old broom;
Not knowing where to sweep.

Climax Change

You may know me, watchful one, by my alias
Old Man, Buccaneer, Water Strider, Bilious
Busted Monometer of Planetary Celsius.
No? Go fuck yourself. I'm listening to Delius,
"On Hearing the First Cuckoo in Spring," envious
Of ovenbirds, swallows, swifts, clamorous canaries; furious
At the soft-bedded shale and its gaseous
Nonlethal vapors. I'm not laughing. I'm hilarious.
I have a problem, *it* does, *they* do, you, him, I, us,
All creatures craven and judicious
Having departed in kayaks and fuming Kias.
Has it not been foretold, Leviticus, lascivious
One?—The way you bade us kneel, twisted like a Mobius
Belt, before insinuating your noxious
Nectar—omnivorous, odoriferous, officious
Orifice-filler, you. In a previous
Proxy you descended, empty charioteer, to query us
On our outerwear's whereabouts. Think on it, Rufous-
Headed woodpecker, use your barbed brain, be suspicious
Of high motives as you crown the dead tree as
Who comes to your rescue? Not I. Unconscious
Tremors, climbing the coils of the virtuous
Time-worn wooden flesh, leave me be. "Witty Is
As Witty Does," sings the sorry fellow atop his egg. Hush.
He'll sit through anything. As in days of yore, he is
Blooming, blazing, withering with his prize zinnias.

Dress Up

You must don your hat
Else spillage occur
From your heat source,
Fanning a draft.
       Don your hat, Sir!

You must dab your eye.
Your duct issue
Gives you away, if you
Must know why
       You must wield a tissue.

Your muffler is knotted
Improperly, Mister,
Emitting a guttural whisper.
Or is that honking not it?
       You want a proper duster.

I don't take well to
Your jagged muffs.
Good man, these ragged cliffs
Shall bid old dressings adieu.
       Take them off.

Your zipper is caught,
You say? You might try
The crowbar nigh.
True, it's roughly wrought,
       As are we.

Button your collar,
Old boy, be a good noose,
Don't refuse.
You were born a bawler.
            Is that news?

Such shame to freeze a digit,
Uncle, or two, when you
Are already shy a few.
You must not drop your mitt
            In this utter zero.

My woe, your sled
Has a loose slat.
Many have pierced a belly like that
Or dented a head.
            Then what?

Buckle up, elder child.
Secure your suspenders,
Restrain your tender
Parts, prepare for wild
            Surrender.

And if you must empty
Your bladder or sac,
Turn down the block,
Seek out the sea;
  Quick, turn back.

Turn back, my lord, you must
Once more.
It's winter.
You've not yet crossed
  The World entire.

You'll need your heavy socks.
The toes are crucial.
This chill is unusual.
I've lost your tracks
  In the floury fuel.

You must lace up your boot.
You've a thing to find
In the wind.
You must be dressed for it.

Creek

I suppose I shan't go fishing
Pa, for fear of finding
We're no fishers,
Our folk, for all our bent
For fish scraps and our
Tolerance for muck dwellers and the like.

This creek is like no other, Pa,
Inky cold and familiar,
Don't drink from it, it
Commands, don't kneel, don't stare down

Or wash in it, don't pry your shoes from off
Your battered stubs, not yet, no jay
Flashes past and asks how you mean
To ask a shit creek to provide.

You exist. It would, too. It falls through
These viney half-corrupted patches of nettled hickory and oak
Into a muddy slough
Into a culvert, splitting

Around the treatment plant
Then joining itself back in a ramrod concrete
Channel beneath pavement;
Then into the lake, sludge, great
Lake.

Do you follow? It's taking you somewhere, it matters
Not where, Pa, it's a trip
At your command, inaudible.

It's the postponed one
We would have scheduled in these winding down days
Together had we not been
What we made of us.
In the stagnant north woods.
In the pale thick end-of-knowing daylight.

Homer

I'm a little muddy today. I dropped in the mud.
My feet came out from me. I know I should
Lose these antique cleats, but sometimes it's good
To grind unwieldy things beneath one's tread
Down to a fine film. As such, I wonder what you'd
Call the goop dribbling from my mouth and head
Accompanying these, how say you, "thoughts"?—Blood?
No, that comes from the ass, where flowers breed
In the fertile loamy waste-dream in the sod.
Let's change the subject. I saw a fine film, *Hud*,
The other sleepless night, and though I would
Not recall it, not a jot, it featured
A father—an old rancher, Homer—his maid
Alma, and a bad kid, Hud, name symbolizing naught,
Who might have been the furtive bastard
Child of the brother (Norman) he detested.
Said Hud: "My Mama loved me then she died."
Amen. Fist fights ensued, malaise, greed, fraud,
Bad faith, threats, laziness, fondness for a slut,
Fugitive speech, agitation, blackout.
Nature itself was become a seamy cult
As some trespassing Mexican cows had spread
Foot-and-mouth disease, and now the boss's herd
Was quarantined—lowing—none would be spared.
In this the family sorrow was mirrored.
Something burned. Something fell from a ledge
Into a hot slender trough. Something (Hud)
Heard menacing voices calling from abroad
    ng a brisk, ungovernable deed.

Before the reel ended we would be plied
With pills and liquor, bound to a post, stuffed
In the shed by a relative (Norman), made
To beg for water, cursed, kicked, spat on, splashed
With battery acid, concussed, left for dead.
The camera zoomed out on an empty road
Over which circled the semblance of a bird.
That was the plot. That was what happened.
It was based, as are all things, on the *Iliad*.
Ending with the repatriation to fairer fields
Of our cattle, which had been hastily interred
On unholy ground, with a stolen spade,
Having lingered a long night in no-man's land,
If cattle we were, my boy, if this were mud.

Employment

Another day come, add it
To the list, the
Not to do list.
Son of mine,
I was rambling across the undercarpeting
Strewn with imperceptible tacks
When a pain rang out in my flank
And I fell to,
But who should answer but no one.
I lost good cause that day, don't ask,
Let us sit a bit in this ill-starred
Suit in the form-filling
Chamber of subtraction,
Listing.
I haven't another trip around the sun
Left in me, vague one,
Son, speak to me.
This is where it thickens,
Me here and it there and me there and them here
And you with the soul.
I'll cross that gravid boneyard
All the day poking
Radishes for remembrance.
This is a private matter
Between a man and his scaffolding
And it shall remain so
Privation permitting.

Procession

From a corner of my bedroom window I could make out
plainly the traffic rising out of the lake and making
its way north towards me up Bathurst Street, first a heavy
black unbroken line of it, and then—as the sun spun out
of the puzzling clouds and sent down its spray—
a jittery lurching tread of grays and yellowed purples, a
vision of squat buses leaning to one side, idling dumpsters,
low-slung open-backed delivery vans lit with graffiti,
flatbeds, excavators, mixers, graders, scrapers,
and tucked among them the nearly buried shadows
of passenger cars, their windshields whitened with noon,
impossible to see into the glare, and there were motorcycles
careering in and around and alongside in looping chrome,
and even some hulking old steel bicycles cloaked in gold
reflective tape, and the fluttering star-shaped outlines of men or boys
straining to push grocery carts—dollies—faltering wooden barrows
heaped with blackened copper fittings, plastic tubing secured
by lengths of hacked rubber, and what looked to be
farm refuse, sheathes of straw and yellowed leaves
bundled hastily, and braided into the traffic's deeper recesses
was an awkward horde of walkers, shouldering duffels
or old canvas packs, or even pillow cases weighted
down with whatever necessities, or bearing nothing at all, proceeding
haltingly in smudgy little blots, leaning on the hatches
of slow-moving trucks and pulling against door handles
or making a futile grab to flag down vehicles that
seemed almost to drive through them without stopping,
and beyond the packs of walkers there were those who walked alone,

too numerous to track, and each one's eyes were fixed to the ground
measuring their strides, as now and then they knelt to pry something
from the heel of their boots, a nub of rocky glass or a nail that pierced
through almost to the flesh, and some walkers
moved crookedly in mismatched shoes, feet
inward-turned, the toes of one foot curled in
and reddened with blisters, and some walkers
had lengths of board tied to their feet with twine, bits
of plank or stripped pine scavenged from barns,
remnants of floorboard or vinyl tile, and the feet
of others were wrapped in bolts of cloth, torn-down
drapes, old rough patchwork skirts, hand towels, t-shirts, even
thin stretched-out socks sewn raggedly together to form a new one,
and some were swaddled in cardboard or newsprint
and many walkers were plainly barefoot and tottered
stiffly on their sores. This I watched, caravan
approaching as a single brilliant being in all its spattered pieces
spread beneath the now arrested sun, harshly clear
like a bleached overexposed photo or x-ray,
and it labored forth in a sluggish swell, compressing, then
flattening out and swelling again, narrowly pinched
at one point and flaring elsewhere, threatening
to disperse then re-forming as a strictly drawn
geometric wedge, insect-like, and as it got closer to me
the lake behind it dried up and was cut from the frame,
and the tremor which I had taken for something in my own body
became a steadier stauncher humming underfoot,
then a harsh unsteady pulse, then the few

trees on the lawn beneath me heaved and swayed
as a long branch was sheared off one and stunned the ground.
I stood in my seventh-floor window taking in what I could
of the sequence, I gathered the surge would close in on me
as I looked on, would reach me where I stood
and I would be called to join it as I had once been called long ago,
not ready for it then and no more so now.
The front edge of the column came to a crossroads
a few blocks from me and suddenly halted, confused,
seemingly repelled, turning on itself in place then seeping sideways
like a pair of unfurling wings east and west along Eglinton Avenue,
past the grocer and druggist and auto body shop and rail depot in
one direction, past the academy and playing fields and bank
and medical offices in the other, and as it came over me
that the mass was spilling away from me
of course I nearly collapsed with relief
tinged somehow with disappointment. Still I watched
the line fanning out, and as it thinned to the edges
of nonexistence I made out, finally, you and the boy
in the intersection, hesitant, bewildered, only the two
of you continued to inch towards me up Bathurst,
you were grasping the boy's hand, he was limping, your hair
had grown long and tangled, the boy had a gash
on his arm or perhaps—I was seized by the thought—his arm is
missing, or some fingers on his left hand are,
and as I sat against the cold windowsill and waited
for you to mount the elevator or the fire stairs—
if the boy was too fearful of the elevator

it would take some time to get up to me—
I could hear the dim echo of your steps in the stairwell
over the cigarette butts and smoke-scarred empties,
and I hoped the vagrants who often sheltered there
bartering junk and scrapping for food
would move aside for you, that your strength
would hold out even if you carried the boy
the last few flights, until you turned down the hall
and the shuttered door of my unit, number 704,
would be pried open and a wind would gust into
my rooms as you and the boy crossed
over and called for me.
I turned. I set my eyes on you.
You were more beautiful than I recalled, the pair of you.
You called for me again, in your two voices,
you kept calling. I had my eyes directly on you.
I couldn't move towards you as you know
nor could I use sound to answer you.
You kept calling. You moved past me,
a form of straining light, yet still you failed
to locate me in the pantry or hardware closet or
in the room where crates of clothes and scribbled-on
papers had been piled or behind the cabinet
or lying in the bath in filmy water.
And as you slowed down your search
room to room and no longer returned
to the rooms you found vacant and gave in and finally
lowered yourself into my chair

you were joined by the boy, half on your lap,
unworried by my absence,
you and the boy, the pair of you,
it was time for your rest,
and no more worried was I,
for I had no more business in this life.

3

Mars

That was a long one. I'll keep this one short.
I'll go one further. I'll quicken this
to a streaking crescent of side-swiping bliss
that will have barely happened.
By the time you have lowered
yourself into the scalding
bath and been brazed by
sudden knowing
this will be done.
Then what? Longing?
Silence? What is silence?
—Then comes the long
hobble home with no tracking tool,
nothing but a regimen of tedious lifts and bends,
roll-overs and hours spent face up
examining the galloping shapes of clouds.
Re-entry goes on long and slow
stretching time to kill it. What were we
doing here all along anyway
supporting life? Surely there were
other planets for us—be reasonable, there
are—where we can take care of each other
in some version of an instant then
thankfully flame out.

Messenger

Perhaps I've gone on long enough so far
but I'm a willing subject who savors
a threesome, some trinity, you say, a wind
trio culled from the local conservatory,
a triplex topped by a nest of defunct
wiring, a three-legged dog. So,
I was daring to say
when hastily I halted,
I had pulled to a three-way stop, my throat in my heart,
when a small tractor rammed me from behind
into a Harley, whose rider parachuted
through my moonroof into my
sticky glass-encrusted lap
with force to make me new.
Does that ring false?—It's false-false-true.
For truly, on an August afternoon much like today
in 1994 I arrived on Second Avenue from far-off parts
in my man-child's suit at the very moment
a bicycling messenger came upon a stopped-short taxi
and missiled through its rear windshield.
At least his head did. The rest was meat
on the hot ground and a passenger with a goring
stain in his midsection who washed
the pavement with tears and vomit.
There was no man to hold.
I stood in place beneath the flashing sun
and turned away and turned watching
and stood turning and here you find me
staring you down across the meridian

having given up all
permanence to speech.
Listener, onlooker, dim-starred crypto-pornographer, I
cannot hide what I witnessed that day
in my throat and mind and in my hot
vestigial self.

Book

I lost my book. It's got the names in it.
Names for things and goods; structures,
Types, boundaries, procedures, goads.
My girl is in it, she who carried it
Within her like a rare worm
Until the untended bird came
And tore its leaves from her
As she lay there,
Pencil pressing page,
Taking it all down.
Then the vast storehouses came down too,
And the small secret ones,
The shelves and grappling hooks,
Dust, ink, lead, linen, ragged board.
It's time to go home and wash up.
Home was in the book in my possession
When I was reading what had been put down
In her hand and mine,
Instructions, inventories,
Names.
But I can't read this while looking at words
While I am assigned to living
In what is called a home.
It is all unkept.
Its yard has turned back to heat-giving
Snail-like deposits drowning in daylight

By the mossed-over fence post.
We lived here once?
We took words down for all the names,
Made markings?
That book is lost, reader,
Not misplaced.

Mower

I don't like the odds. I don't know them
but a little polymer tube
inside me collecting information
tells me I could do better
at another job, for instance
being a bone.
Then I might allow myself a long stay
in the crust subjected
to ungodly pressures until my microgram
of carbon leaches out and gets put
to use in a, for instance,
lawn machine. Those odds I like.
I see you out back tending yard
rather tending the hot hard yellow
straw-covered patch and I know
I shall live in your memory a numb
instant before you cut me down
keeping the blade clean
in the aperture between us.
You never were much for slots.
Or for the wheel, or craps,
or the ponies, or 3-2-1, and I have
caught you at the bridge table
taking a hand of rummy
with the old lady and letting
her get away with one.
I take it was an act of mercy
for I recall she was being eaten
with tumors and one would have her take

some token along for the long
slump, along
with sexual need and meals gone cold and cash-
starved panic all interred for someday's
fossil gorge. I know like every boy you loved
your mother as she pushed her manual
mower over the fenced-off
sloping inch of sod,
but what were the odds, what were the odds?
It takes cold calculation
to be eternal, as the blind rust-colored
dirt-moving beetles are in their
pure submission to fact.
I'm one to talk. I'm one who
will take the temple down on himself
so his rubble may be memorial
to all who come to build stone tools
in the dark regressive days to come.

Waterfall

I would use these words but for
Once there was something inside me
A pebble, part of one
White beam spilling
Headlong through the darkening
Gates

Waterfall, where was I

Scrambled up the loose flinty scree
Forcing an opening through the brush
A jeep trail narrowing
To a skid trail, washboarded, overgrown
With generations of rough leaves
To a ghost trail
A hunter might have cut
Tracking a particular bloodied
Many-pointed buck up the scarp
Past the hunter's turnaround
Past the discarded animal
God knows to the source
Muddy unreflective trickle wanting
To leave this world

I mean the busted spigot
In the room beyond
I mean the light I licked up
To get to the ferny cloud-cracked pool
Forgetting

Now look at my mirror
I'm an old bugger in a potted grove
While the sun allows it
Before the sun prohibits it

Waterway, where are you

Fuck. Nothing tells me what to do
Except the feeder tells me to
Put the little spoon in and chew
And I've lost the will to
So it rests there, wanting swallowing
Yet I would not want it
Yet still I want it if it will have me

Pinned to a painted rock
A goldfinch wings past
Disappearing into
The great cascade

I wade in
And wash without help
In the spring-fed cold
And the flow of it
Rubs me away

Keeper

It's outside time. It's time to charge
Outside into the alternating currents.

It's inside time. The chair has readied itself
For the favor of your deadweight.

Time is down at the memory factory
On the assembly floor of time's machinery,

Belts, gears, levers, prongs, the guts and gore
Of your stomped-on unrecovered timepiece.

Don't look on it. It may call to mind a time
We paused in white rain

In mazy boreal woods. We'll get back there
In time, never finding a way out once we're in.

Time tells me we were once too young to be
Ripe as the world required. It took time to harden,

Took the efforts of time's army
Keeping watch over our compound for a time

As you watch over me in perpetuity. No one
Forces you, waster of it, lapser, keeper,

Standing across my tiles in the mean-
Time within the sheared curtains staring

Hard at my chair for an ounce of light.
Hard time. Endurance.

Baby

He's getting so big.
In no time he will topple over.

In no time he will outgrow his soft
Sandals and go forth ever barefooted.

He narrows his eyes into focus, coming through
The blur to make out things and people,

The back of his spoon, a dove's shadow, sun spots,
Vaguely sunken bones in mother's chest

As she breathes away from him.
Soon it will be all his ripe eyes see.

Now he's putting sounds together
That shall be blended into words someday.

—Let him, while his sounds have something to say
Not altogether unintelligible.

He's learning to count, higher, higher, until
He's nearly nothing

Unencumbered, nearly
Infinite.

He scampers and climbs and keens and kicks himself
Free of bedclothes. Sleep awaits him. As in dream,

May he come to recall petting the visitor's dog
In the long-gone years no one touches him

And when he touches himself
May the whisper in his nerve endings not subside.

Let it keep him awake at night,
Rousing him, as we would, in the darkened room.

As far as he knows he was never not held by us.
Let him hold onto that.

Unemployment

Out of cash, out of well-fitting trousers,
Out of soap and apples,
Out of pencils, out of my keeper's
Reach.

I wish to set myself afire
But may not. This morning
(Last night) in the common room
I watched the administration
Of oxygen to one who had none

And I would not sit down, demanding
To do so.

Later I happened on a man
At the piano, and though I have happened five or six times
On men at the piano,
None moved his hand like this
Within the keys.

I sat beside him, looking for a sound
A chest sound. Not listening; I don't listen
Anymore. I make music
But I don't listen.

Trans

Third and long.
A poem of distance.
A picture window giving on a black maple,
a squat Yeshiva and an embankment
on which transcontinental traffic whirs.
I need assistance in the matters
of routine existence, if you will,
like gripping a ball or cleaning my ass,
like getting down field or knowing my name.
It's not important I know my name
as long as I know yours.
And you are, you are, you are, you are.
I can find my way out of here and back
in the absence of landmarks, past an acre
of identical doors, garage doors,
patio doors, rectangular doorways, shafts
of dormant ruined light, for I
have my place here, absent though I am,
though on reflection you are nowhere
where I left you.
You might have left early
which I can appreciate.

71

Harp

We can't do this longer
our mind, what is it, is a worn
garment we can peer through to the pond beyond
when we peer through its dross with unmoving eye.
We're in trouble, mortal.
The landlord wants us out,
and all our furnishings,
paper plates, apple cores,
and all our pissed-in soda bottles,
and all our nightly pleadings.
We touched a girl, they tell us,
you can't remove that from us,
when no one was looking in the telescope
where we were caught, climbing
to the lookout, stepping into
her blear. It's been so long
it's the very idea
of touch that gives grief.

AND SO
for failure to perform our obligations
under the contract that binds us
we must be taken from this property
AND SO
when the man shows up
with his carnival of restraints
he must find us packed in our bathrobe,
terry cotton, standard issue

AND WHEN the crease is parted
the animal inside shall be deemed
a few tufts of musty tissue
through which sings a wind.

Departure

That was a departure for me
I should know, having once parted
flame from its dying coal
while crossing, barefoot, the furthest beach.
That wasn't who I would have taken to be me, but
I did it for no reason other than I loved
to endure, and loved things, like sand,
in the last light of their worn majesty.
I watched a winged thing take off
over the waters and fall into the circumference,
completing it. Back then I wore a new dress
each of my outings, checks, ovals,
bloody florals on my wanderings in the garden
to bring fresh plantings back to you,
to bring stems to your side.
Where had you gone? You gave no address
but the one you spoke and I mistook
for a resting place in the long row
of identical one-season awnings.
That's how I take it we got into this hole,
coming together with parted lips
from which you put forth parting sounds.
"To hell with it," you said, because
it was true you said it, because
by then you had seen the fire for what it is.

Tandem

I still dream, I think
though you might not think to look
inside me. In this one, I think
you were still seated with the boy
behind me on a long bicycle
as I rode across a narrow unsteady
jerry-rigged footbridge of sorts
—warped planks skimming the shallow
scudded surface of a pond,
bricks and ruddy little boulders
and rough-cut logs and bundles of prickly reeds
trying to fill the gaps like mortar.
I wondered if the boy was frightened by the clouds
of noiseless green and gold dragonflies
pinging against me,
speckling me with a rash of reddish dots.
Otherwise, all was painless.
The pond was enclosed from whatever lay beyond
by a tangle of wild hedges and by the long hanging
branches of moss-topped oaks.
I rode slowly. Water splashed up at me
blurring but I pinched one eye shut
and stared with the other towards the far shore
as through an eyepiece
as I held myself rigid
and wrangled the bicycle towards balance.
It seemed impossible. The bicycle was so
heavy my legs barely turned and I rode so
slowly on the slick planks I envisioned myself

toppling sideways and submerging the three of us.
You know how dreams are, or used to be.
Then suddenly I was leaning in, almost at land,
suddenly my front wheel reached land
and the touch of it was elating,
like landing in the grasp of a long-gone
lover or parent who had, it seemed, been there
all along waiting for you to wake.
Then I turned to you and the boy, rather
the dream turned. For the bicycle had somehow
cracked apart behind me, you and the boy
had been split from the bicycle
and were now dragging yourselves
on the makeshift bridge as it sank
into the muck and as you struggled forward
your clothes were torn and you were
filthy and winded but somehow
very calm as though that was the crossing
you expected or that was the way
one crosses. And then you were lost to me
and the boy was lost, too.

I know it is dull being told
another's dream, even if the dream
involves you and you had lost faith
the person could still dream or
otherwise think or want, but I think
I was then in a kind of library,

a place, at least, encased in shelves,
and a volume lay open
in front of me and I looked
on pretending to read
columns of script, rigorous precise
technical grammar of numeric
codes, half-moons, inverted triangles.
Then a clacking startled me from behind.
It was you, as you must know, having found me
after your long search, your legs were scratched
and you had a terrible bruise on your
left shoulder and that arm hung
at your side unmoving.
I shut the book abruptly and
it must have seemed I was putting something
from your eyes, words in my own hand you
needed to know and had come
specifically in search of.
And I could not say to you—
because I physically could not
speak, as it is true I cannot—
that what I was hiding from you was
not any words of mine but rather
my actual lack of them,
of symbol-stained pages
of interior legible human text.
You pulled the book from me, you were riffling
the pages with some urgency

until you found your page and set to reading
with an absorption that made all else recede.
Indeed I was then at a remove, looking on
from some distant enclosure
in the woods on the pond's far side, perhaps
a bird blind or a hunter's rotted tree stand,
and you were very small, a few pencil
strokes suggesting a body,
as you read to the boy
in that faint reedy beautiful voice
I once knew, until the boy grew drowsy
and leaned his head against you
and shut his eyes as you kept reading.

That was my dream, my love,
it is what I have left to tell you—you
whom I love with the last breath
of nothing left inside me.

ACKNOWLEDGMENTS

Grateful acknowledgment to the publications in which these poems have appeared:

Boston Review, The Claudius App, Company, Denver Quarterly, Fence, Harvard Review, Iowa Review, jubilat, Lana Turner, PEN Poetry Series, Poetry, and *Poetry Northwest.*

Emily Wilson and Spurwink Press published a broadside of "Cave." Wolfram Swets and Tungsten Press published broadsides of "Baby" and "Harp," and a chapbook edition of "Tandem."

Mark Levine has published three books of poems, *Debt* (1993), *Enola Gay* (2000) and *The Wilds* (2006), and a book of nonfiction, *F5* (2007). He has also written journalism for many magazines, including *The New Yorker*, *The New York Times Magazine*, and *Outside*. He has received fellowships from the Canada Council for the Arts, the National Endowment for the Arts, and the Whiting Foundation. He teaches at the Iowa Writers' Workshop.

Publication of this book was made possible by grants and donations.

We are also grateful to those individuals who participated in our 2015 Build a Book Program. They are:

Jan Bender-Zanoni, Betsy Bonner, Deirdre Brill, Carla & Stephen Carlson, Liza Charlesworth, Catherine Degraw & Michael Connor, Greg Egan, Martha Webster & Robert Fuentes, Anthony Guetti, Hermann Hesse, Deming Holleran, Joy Jones, Katie Childs & Josh Kalscheur, Michelle King, David Lee, Howard Levy, Jillian Lewis, Juliana Lewis, Owen Lewis, Alice St. Claire Long & David Long, Catherine McArthur, Nathan McClain, Carolyn Murdoch, Tracey Orick, Kathleen Ossip, Eileen Pollack, Barbara Preminger, Vinode Ramgopal, Roni Schotter, Soraya Shalforoosh, Marjorie & Lew Tesser, David Tze, Abby Wender, and Leah Nanako Winkler.

perpetully perpetreal
perpetreaton

primate

mary

boreal

Oob

wet
air sprtizes woke jonah &1
1/2 up last night —
could close the
window but didn't.
I liked it.